Dinosaur Alphabet

Peter Riley

Oxford

Oxford University Press, Great Clarendon Street, Oxford, OX2 6DP

Oxford New York
Athens Auckland Bangkok Bogota Buenos Aires
Calcutta Cape Town Chennai Dar es Salaam Delhi
Florence Hong Kong Istanbul Karachi Kuala Lumpur
Madrid Melbourne Mexico City Mumbai Nairobi Paris
São Paulo Singapore Taipei Tokyo Toronto Warsaw

and associated companies in
Berlin Ibadan

Oxford is a trade mark of Oxford University Press

ISBN 0 19 915562 3
Available in packs
Animals Pack of Six (one of each book)   ISBN 0 19 915567 4
Animals Class Pack   (six of each book)   ISBN 0 19 915618 2

Acknowledgements

The Publisher would like to thank The Natural History Museum for
permission to reproduce the photograph on p 3.

Main illustrations by Christopher Tomlin
Cartoons by Pat McCarthy c/o J Martin & Artists
Plant and bone symbols by Brett Breckon

With special thanks to Dr Kevin Padian, University of Berkeley, California

Printed in Hong Kong

Introduction

Dinosaurs were animals that lived a long time ago. This book will tell you about a dinosaur for every letter of the alphabet.

A dinosaur fossil

These symbols tell you what a dinosaur ate.

 Plants

 Animals

A Apatosaurus

When an ***Apatosaurus*** walked its feet thumped the ground and made a sound like thunder.

Apatosaurus' leg bones were 2m long. ▼

4

B Baryonyx

Baryonyx means heavy claw.
This dinosaur had a claw on
each front foot and
used the claws
to catch fish.

claw

C Chasmosaurus

This dinosaur had a frill around its neck. The frill showed other dinosaurs it was fierce.

The frill was made of horn.

D Diplodocus

This dinosaur's tail bones had two spikes which stuck out. They helped the dinosaur balance.

The bones looked like this.

Edmontosaurus

Edmontosaurus had a beak like a duck and lots of teeth. Its teeth were shaped like diamonds.

diamond

tooth

7

F Fabrosaurus

Fabrosaurus stood on its toes to run away.

G Gallimimus

Gallimimus looked like a very large bird.

Herrerasaurus

Herrerasaurus was one of the first dinosaurs.
It used its front feet to catch
animals to eat.

I Iguanodon

Iguanodon had hooves on its fingers and toes. It ate plants on the ground.

hooves

J Jubbulpuria

Jubbulpuria ran quickly to catch small animals to eat.

K Kentrosaurus

Kentrosaurus means spiky lizard. It had spikes along its back.

spikes

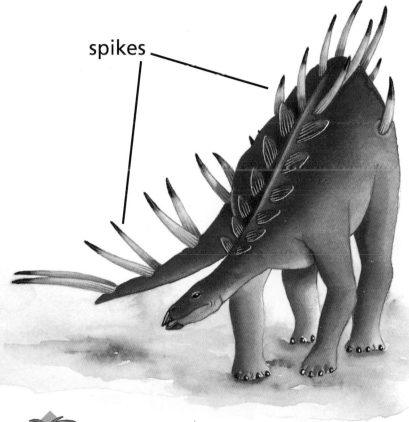

L Lambeosaurus

This dinosaur had a crest on its head. **Lambeosaurus** blew into its crest to make a sound like a trumpet.

crest

M Maiasaura

Maiasaura means good
mother lizard. The mother
dinosaur was good at
looking after the young
dinosaurs.

N Nodosaurus

Nodosaurus means lumpy
lizard. The lumps on its
skin protected it when
it was attacked.

Oviraptor

Oviraptor stole other dinosaurs' eggs from their nests.

Oviraptor used a spiky bone in its mouth to break the eggs. ▼

spiky bone

Pentaceratops

Pentaceratops means five-horned lizard.
This dinosaur used its horns
to protect itself.

horn

Quaesitosaurus

R # Riojasaurus

Quaesitosaurus had a long neck so it could eat tall plants.

Riojasaurus was as long as a coach.

S Stegosaurus

Stegosaurus had plates made of bone on its back. The sun warmed the plates and made the dinosaur warm.

The brain of a Stegosaurus was the same size as a walnut.

Tyrannosaurus rex

Tyrannosaurus rex hunted its own food, and ate animals killed by other dinosaurs.

Gigantosaurus was even bigger than Tyrannosaurus rex. ▼

Ultrasaurus

Ultrasaurus means the biggest lizard. Ultrasaurus was the biggest land animal that ever lived.

▲ Ultrasaurus weighed more than eight elephants.

V Velociraptor

Velociraptor had a huge claw on each foot. It used these claws like knives.

claw

Wannanosaurus

Wannanosaurus fought other dinosaurs by pushing them with its head.

Xuanhanosaurus

This dinosaur's bones were found in Xuanhan in China.

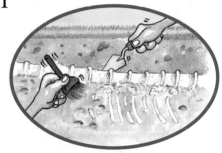

Yunnanosaurus had teeth which were shaped like spoons.

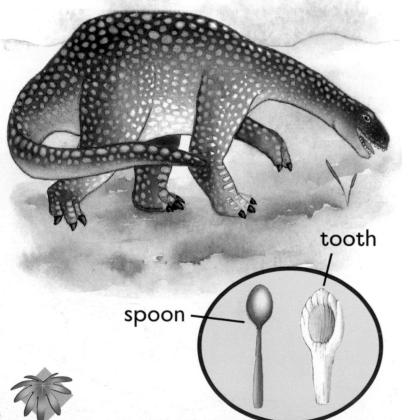

tooth

spoon

Z Zephyrosaurus

The bones of this dinosaur were found in Montana, in the United States.

Did you know?

Dinosaurs lived on the land, but many other animals lived at the same time.

Quezalcoatlus was the largest flying animal of all time.

Pterodactyls flew in the air.

Plesiosaur

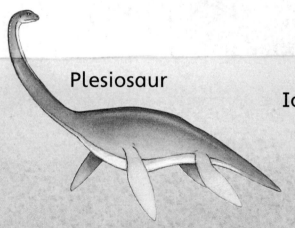

Ichthyosaur

Pliosaur

Mosasaur

Ichthyosaurs, Mosasaurs, Plesiosaurs, and Pliosaurs swam in the sea.

Index